# I WANT TO BE AN AUTHOR
## A step-by-step workbook to guide your child's first story

Lynn Santer: www.LynnSanter.com
Auntie Lynn: www.TheMagicalScarecrows.com

## Introduction

The art of storytelling began long before mankind developed writing tools. It is believed that soon after the skill of language evolved people started telling stories to educate, to entertain and as a means to express their feelings, beliefs and heroism.

Our ancestors probably gathered around the evening fires to be captivated, enchanted and enlightened by the ancient storytellers. Families and communities bonded through stories that connected their imaginations, curiosity and a need to find meaning and explanations for events in their lives.

The long tradition of storytelling is evident in the earliest cultures, such as the Australian Aborigines. Telling stories was also a nurturing act for both the listener and the teller. Those who excelled at storytelling became our entertainers, cultural advisors, educators and historians. The importance of the storyteller in human history cannot be overstated. Storytelling was, and remains, one of the most respected skills a person can master.

The first evidence of storytelling can be found in cave paintings, which recorded both history and mythology in their storylines. Over time, such respect was given to the storytellers that they became honoured members of Royal Courts, Sages and Scribes.

Storytelling can preserve a culture, instil moral values and it can be therapeutic. The art and skill of storytelling has come a long way over human history but three things remain constant and crucial:

**The plot**
**The characters &**
**The narrative**

In this first ever step-by-step guide to teach your child the art of storytelling perhaps we may just be nurturing the next Steven Spielberg, Richard Branson or Plato! In every sphere of human existence, be it entertainment, commerce or philosophy, it all begins with the story...

## About this author

Lynn Santer (also known as "Auntie Lynn") first started writing stories as an infant, on her bedroom wall in crayon. Her parents quickly decided to buy her some writing paper and pencils! She submitted her first story "The Magical Scarecrow" to a publisher when she was only nine years old. Since then she has penned a series of best-selling novels, she has become a much sought-after ghost writer and celebrity biographer and she developed her first story into a philanthropic children range called "The Magical Scarecrows".

Nominated for the Pride of Australia medal in 2008, in recognition of her work, Lynn moved into film production and soon won a string of awards for her short films and feature screenplays. Today she has several major projects in development in Hollywood while she resides by a peaceful lake on the Gold Coast of Australia.

STORYLINE

# step 1

## PICK A SUBJECT

_____

Your story could be about animals, dreams, family, space battles... anything you like.

# step 2

## PICK A GENRE

This could be drama, comedy, SciFi, adventure... anything you like.

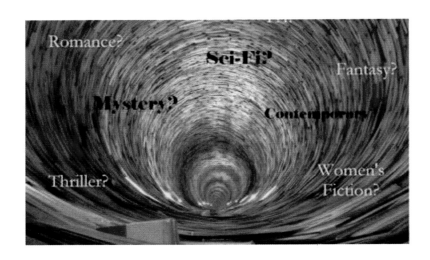

Now it starts getting interesting because you are going to choose your characters!!!

Characters can be real or imagined but we have to have a goodie, a baddie and a confidante (friend).

What are your characters' names?

Are they girls, boys, animals or imagined creatures?

What makes them good or bad or maybe funny?

Do they have particular things they always say, for example:  "I dunno" or "for crying out loud" or anything you like.

Write down your characters names and a brief description about them on the next pages.

# THE GOODIE

# THE BADDIE

_____

_____

_____

_____

_____

_____

_____

_____

_____

_____

_____

_____

# THE CONFIDANTE (Friend)

_____

_____

_____

_____

_____

_____

_____

_____

_____

_____

_____

# WHAT IS AT STAKE?

_____

In every successful story something is "at stake". Is your GOODIE looking for buried treasure? Maybe he or she is trying to save someone from the BADDIE. Maybe he or she is trying to be the best at something? Think of all the stories you have enjoyed the most and try to remember what was at stake in those stories. Maybe you can write a story like one of those.

Write down some ideas about what might be at stake in your story here:

_____

_____

_____

_____

_____

_____

_____

_____

_____

_____

_____

## WHAT IS THE CATALYST?

The catalyst is something that happens near the beginning of the story which sends the GOODIE on the journey of the story to achieve a goal... to succeed in whatever it is that is at stake in your story. It could be the discovery of an ancient map, or maybe someone is making fun of them at school, or maybe they had an accident and have been told they can never do something again and they set out to prove that they can.

The catalyst can be anything you like but what is important is that whatever the catalyst is, it sends the GOODIE on a journey and into a world which is not like anything they have known before. In this way your GOODIE can grow as they experience the journey of the story. This is called a CHARACTER ARC.

In every successful story the GOODIE must confront something to emerge at the end of the story a different, bigger, better, more successful person than they were at the start because they have learned things and/or achieved things along the way.

The catalyst is what drives your story forward into the main action.

NOTE: "Protagonist" is the professional storyteller's word for the GOODIE.

Catalyst

- The Catalyst is an event in the story that LAUNCHES the story into motion, regardless if the Protagonist is ready for it or not. A decision is made, and it forces a decision by the Protagonist. Regardless the story is forced onward!

Write down some ideas for what the catalyst might be in your story here:

_____

_____

_____

_____

_____

_____

_____

_____

_____

_____

# WHAT DOES THE WORLD OF YOUR STORY LOOK LIKE?

Is your story set in the past, present or future? Is it set on earth, under the sea or in outer space? Is your story set in school or in a mythical world of monsters and dragons? Is there magic in the world of your story or is your story setting more "real world"?

Decide what "The World" of your story might look like and make some notes on the next page.

Write down some ideas about what the world of your story looks like here:

_____

_____

_____

_____

_____

_____

_____

_____

_____

_____

## Never forget to drop breadcrumbs!

Something else that all successful stories do is to "drop breadcrumbs". This means that early in the story your GOODIE might see something, or learn something, or meet someone who is going to be useful or important to them as the story progresses. What might some of your breadcrumbs be?

_____

_____

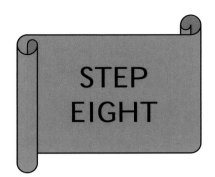

## EVERY STORY MUST HAVE A BEGINNING, A MIDDLE AND AN END

Perhaps that sounds very obvious but you would be surprised how many first time authors make a mistake in this vital part of the story structure.

In fact, it is more important to know where you want your story to finish before you begin than it is to imagine your beginning.

When you know where it is you want your story to finish, then everything you do before the end will be leading towards where you know the story is heading. It's like heading out on a road trip - you have to know where you're going to be able to map your journey. It's the same with a story.

Is there going to be a big battle at the end of your story? A triumphant race to victory? The discovery of buried treasure? Winning the admiration of your peers? How would you like to see your story conclude?

Write down some ideas about how your story might finish here:

_____

_____

_____

_____

_____

_____

_____

_____

_____

_____

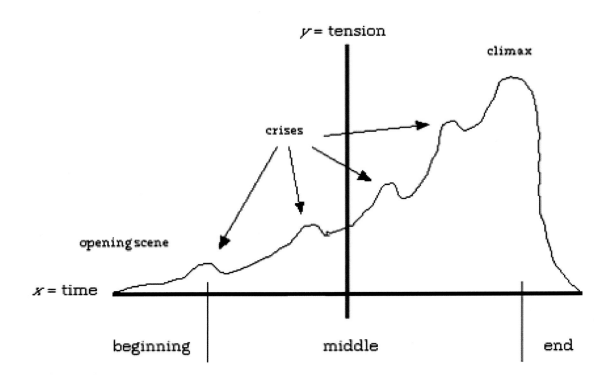

 **The Character Arc**

In Step Five we talked about the catalyst for your story and making the "character arc" (that is showing how your GOODIE character grows from the beginning of the story to the end). To achieve a character arc, a character must confront what they fear most to achieve their goal (the thing that is at stake in your story).

Let me give you a very simple example...

Let's say there is a puppy in a pound or rescue shelter. Let's say there is a fire. The puppy, very understandably, becomes terrified of fire. The puppy says to himself that if he is ever rescued he will be so grateful he will do anything to protect the person who rescues him. This establishes the puppy as the GOODIE character, or protagonist.

One day a young boy adopts the puppy from the pound. That is the catalyst that sends the puppy into a whole new world.

Together the boy and the puppy go on lots of adventures and form a firm friendship.

Over the years the puppy grows into a dog and the boy becomes a teenager. The puppy never forgets the promise he made to himself when he was in the pound. What is at stake for the puppy, now a dog, is to prove to himself and those in his world that he is loyal and will always be grateful for being rescued.

Throughout their adventures in the story the puppy may have demonstrated his loyalty in many ways but along the way he has always shied away from fire. Maybe we could have seen this when he was nervous near a campfire, or when he barked at someone lighting a gas stove.

There are lots of ways of showing how your character feels in storytelling. In this example, though, near the end of the story there is an unexpected twist...

The teenager is caught in a house fire. The only way the dog can save the person who once saved him is to face his biggest fear of all - fire.

Throughout the story we thought he would never overcome his fear of fire because we'd seen him shy away from it so many times.

Now, however, he has to face his biggest fear or lose the person who means the most to him while at the same time not honouring the promise he made to himself.

Here's a secret about storytelling. In storytelling you can make absolutely anything happen that you want. We might all share the puppy's fear of fire. It's only natural and sensible to be afraid of fire - it's dangerous! This isn't really about facing fire, however.

What you are doing when you tell a story this way is using fire as a metaphor (that means describing a one thing to explain another).

What you are saying in your story when your GOODIE confronts their fear to achieve their goal, is that the goal is more important than their fear. Because the goal is more important than their fear they will do something that we (the reader/audience of your story) would not have believed they could do to achieve that goal. In facing a fear your character grows and becomes more than we ever thought possible. That's a character arc.

IT DOES NOT MEAN YOU SHOULD GO AND RUN INTO A FIRE TO PROVE A POINT IN REAL LIFE!

This is a map of a character arc
(See more about this on page 50)

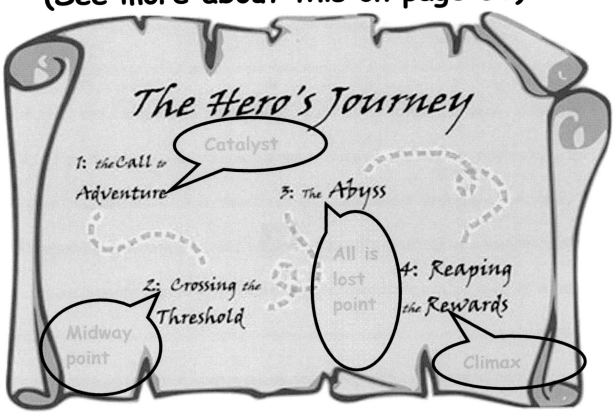

Write down some ideas about what fears your GOODIE might face in your story here:

_____

_____

_____

_____

_____

_____

_____

_____

_____

_____

# THE "ALL IS LOST" POINT (or "Abyss")

In telling you the story about the puppy and the fire we covered another really important aspect of storytelling - the "all is lost" point.

Every successful story has a point, near the end, when just as you thought everything was going well there's a near disaster leading to the final climatic moment (where the GOODIE will stop at nothing to achieve the goal).

Write down some ideas about what the "all is lost" point might be in your story here:

_____

_____

_____

_____

_____

_____

_____

_____

_____

_____

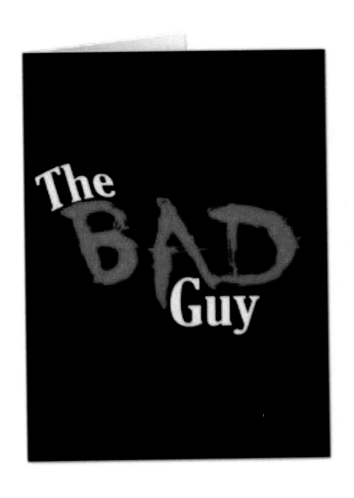

NO GOOD STORY IS A GOOD STORY
WITHOUT A REALLY BAD
BAD GUY!

The reason we have bad guys is to show how good our good guys can be. The bad guys often seem to be smarter, faster, stronger and/or wealthier than the good guys... but that's what makes the good guy's victory so rewarding. If the challenge was easy, the good guy wouldn't need to be much of a hero to achieve the goal, would they?

In mapping out your story you have to think about all the ways your bad guy can stand in your good guy's way. You should include every obstacle, challenge, threat and danger you can think of for your good guy to face.

Write down some of the ways your bad guy can make things difficult in your story here:

_____

_____

_____

_____

_____

_____

_____

_____

_____

_____

_____

Let's make things REALLY difficult. Write down some more ideas here:

_____

_____

_____

_____

_____

_____

_____

_____

_____

_____

# the Confidante

The role of the confidante, or friend, is probably one of the most overlooked roles for the first time author. While this character may seem minor, he or she is anything but. This character allows our GOODIE to share their hopes, dreams, fears and desires.

This character can also offer some light relief (funny moments when everything has been very dramatic). They can often serve as a mentor (teacher and guide) as well. This is what Obi Wan Kenobi did for Luke Skywalker in "Star Wars". Without Obi Wan's friendship and guidance, Luke would never have become the remarkable Jedi that he did. Obi Wan was also the character who allowed Luke to express his fears and self-doubts (something he would never have done to Hans Solo or Princess Leia).

How will your confidante character help the GOODIE in your story?

_____

_____

_____

_____

_____

_____

_____

_____

_____

_____

_____

# CONFIDANTE

- **Someone in whom the central character confides, thus revealing the main character's personality, thoughts, and intentions.** The confidante does not need to be a person

  - Example: In a story, Melvin Sanders is a detective on the trail of a serial killer. He travels with his pet dog, a pug named Chops. Instead of listening to the radio, Melvin talks to Chops, telling him his theories about the serial killer and his concern he may never discover the killer's identity.

# THE CLIMAX

Once your GOODIE (protagonist/hero) experiences a CATALYST (inciting incident) and the main action begins, there are complications and crisis moments, courtesy of your BADDIE.

In the world of your story, your GOODIE strives to achieve their goal for whatever it is that is at stake. They have left breadcrumbs we have discovered along the way. We reach an "all is lost" point and think: OH NO! Now we have the HOORAY or climax moment, when the character arcs (grows), achieves the goal and receives their just reward as a result. The reward might be an actual award, admiration or it might simply be the knowledge that they have beaten the odds and they feel good about themselves.

This is where we all breath a sigh of relief because it's all worked out the way we wanted.

# Now, you are ready!

There are many, many, MANY more topics to cover on storytelling but for your first attempt this should be enough to get you started.

Next time we can look at things like:


**The midway point**. This is where the GOODIE makes a decision to proceed forward when he could have turned back up until that moment. By the middle of the story a decision is made which raises the dramatic tension and often puts a time critical element in place. The story then becomes "do or die", "sink or swim"... there is NO GOING BACK NOW! This is what we mean by "crossing the threshold" in the character arc map on page 35.

**Foreshadow and payoff**. This is where you plant something at the beginning of the story knowing you are going to use it later. For example, someone may open a drawer and see a key. It doesn't mean anything at the time but later on the GOODIE realises that key will open the door he needs to open to receive a vital clue.

**Conflict**. The main thing that keeps an audience engaged in a story is seeing the GOODIE run into complications, obstacles and confrontations with the bad guy. There are many kinds of conflict we can discuss.

**Sub plots**. This is often, but not always, a romance running behind the main story.

**Motivation**. There are many, many, MANY different types of motivation for your characters we can discuss next time.

Until then...

In writing your story (and in everything in life) remember what Auntie Lynn's Magical Scarecrows always say:

*You are only bound by your imagination...*
*Imagination is boundless!*

THE GREATEST STORY NEVER TOLD IS YOURS

# NOW YOU CAN WRITE YOUR STORY

Remember all the points you've written down so far. Don't worry if you find you are part way through your story and you've forgotten something, or change your mind. That happens to ALL writers, even the very experienced ones!

The journey of a thousand miles begins with the first step. In other words, everyone has to start somewhere and this is where you begin your journey into a world that is entirely of your creation. Enjoy!

Made in the USA
Middletown, DE
14 December 2020

27954505R00046